Grandy's Poems

Edward E. Williams

DORRANCE
PUBLISHING CO
EST. 1920
PITTSBURGH, PENNSYLVANIA 15238

Dorrance Publishing Co
585 Alpha Drive
Pittsburgh, PA 15238
Visit our website at www.dorrancebookstore.com

ISBN: 978-1-6442-6225-2
eISBN978-1-6442-6407-2

Foreword

This is an attempt to convert poems that I wrote from a personal poem to commercially adaptable poem. Now that I have said that, let me tell you that all of the poems that are either Anniversary, Birthday, Mother's Day, Valentine or Christmas types of poems were written to the people that I loved. That would be either my wife, Barbara Ann Johnson Williams; my daughter, Dana Ann Williams Stewart; my granddaughter, Emily Leanne Stewart; or my grandson, Scott Christopher Stewart. Of course, my mind conjured up the words, but not without a tremendous amount of input from my heart. I hope that all of the poems reflect that fact. Notice that the first two poems I made them year specific and gender specific to show how each of the poems could be used.

Also, I would like to acknowledge my granddaughter, Emily Leanne Stewart, and her invaluable assistance in putting this book together. I would probably never have been able to complete this book without her assistance. Thank you, Emily.

Grandy's Poems

Table of Contents

One day someone will come into your life.

They're not a brother, a sister, a husband or a wife.

They will be someone that you don't even know.

But soon a friendship will start to grow.

They will share your hopes, joys, sorrows and fears.

They will also share your laughter and your tears.

You will begin to wonder how did this all begin.

That I was blessed to have you as

MY SPECIAL FRIEND.

Anniversaries

FEMALE VERSION
SILVER ANNIVERSARY

A wedding is a special thing.
It's more than a bridal walk, a kiss and a ring.
It's a commitment for life,
Between a man and his wife.
It's saying that I truly care,
And that I will always be there.
If you laugh, you know that I'll want to hear.
But if you cry, I'll also shed a tear.
I'll try to lift you up, if you are down.
Because I promised I would always be around.
I would expect no less from you.
Because I know you exceed everything that I do.
It's always been that way through our twenty five years of married life.
That's why I chose to be your wife.
Now the time has come to celebrate our Silver Anniversary.
I'm extremely happy that you decided to share these past twenty five years with me.

SILVER ANNIVERSARY 2

Thank you for twenty-five years that I have been your wife,

For the twenty-five years that I shared in your life.

For the twenty-five years that I know that you cared.

For the twenty-five years of joys and sorrows we shared.

Thank you for the twenty-five years of marital bliss.

Made sweeter each day with every kiss.

But of all the things that I've mentioned above.

I thank you most for the Twenty-Five Years of Love.

GOLDEN ANNIVERSARY

A wedding is a special thing,
It's more than a bridal walk, a kiss, and a ring.
It's a commitment for life,
Between a man and his wife.
It's saying that I truly care
And that I will always be there.
If you laugh, you know that I'll want to hear
But if you cry, I'll also shed a tear
I'll try to lift you up, if you are down.
Because I promised I would always be around.
I would expect no less from you.
Because I know you exceed everything that I do.
It's always been that way through our fifty years of married life.
That's why I chose to be your wife.
Now the time has come to celebrate our Golden Anniversary.
I'm extremely happy that you decided
to share these fifty years with me.

GOLDEN ANNIVERSARY 2

Thank you for fifty years that I have been your wife
For the fifty years that I shared in your life.
For the fifty years that I know that you cared.
For the fifty years of joys and sorrows we shared.
Thank you for the fifty years of marital bliss.
Made sweeter each day with every kiss.
But of all the things that I've mentioned above.
I thank you most for the Fifty Years of Love.

ANY YEAR ANNIVERSARY

A wedding is a special thing.
It's more than a bridal walk, a kiss and a ring.
It's a commitment for life,
Between a man and his wife.
It's saying that I truly care
And that I will always be there.
If you laugh, you know that I'll want to hear.
But if you cry, I'll also shed a tear.
I'll try to lift you up, if you are down.
Because I promised I would always be around.
I would expect no less from you.
Because I know you exceed everything that I do.
It's always been that way throughout our married life.
That's why I chose to be your wife.
Now the time has come to celebrate our Anniversary.
I'm extremely happy that you decided to share these years with me.

ANY YEAR ANNIVERSARY 2

Thank you for the years that I have been your wife
For the years that I shared in your life.
For the years that I know that you cared.
For the years of joys and sorrows we shared.
Thank you for the years of marital bliss.
Made sweeter each day with every kiss.
But of all the things that I've mentioned above.
I thank you most for these Years of Love.

MALE VERSION
SILVER ANNIVERSARY

A wedding is a special thing.
It's more than a bridal walk, a kiss and a ring.
It's a commitment for life,
Between a man and his wife.
It's saying that I truly care
And that I will always be there.
If you laugh, you know that I'll want to hear.
But if you cry, I'll also shed a tear.
I'll try to lift you up, if you are down.
Because I promised I would always be around.
I would expect no less from you.
Because I know you exceed everything that I do.
It's always been that way through our twenty-five years of married life.
That's why I chose you to be my precious wife.
Now the time has come to celebrate our Silver Anniversary.
I'm extremely happy that you decided
to share these past twenty-five years with me.

SILVER ANNIVERSARY 2

Thank you for twenty-five years of being my wife

For the twenty-five years that I shared in your life.

For the twenty-five years that I know that you cared.

For the twenty-five years of joys and sorrows we shared.

Thank you for the twenty-five years of marital bliss.

Made sweeter each day with every kiss.

But of all the things that I've mentioned above.

I thank you most for the Twenty-Five Years of Love.

GOLDEN ANNIVERSARY

A wedding is a special thing.
It's more than a bridal walk, a kiss and a ring.
 It's a commitment for life,
Between a man and his wife.
It's saying that I truly care
And that I will always be there.
If you laugh, you know that I'll want to hear.
But if you cry, I'll also shed a tear.
I'll try to lift you up, if you are down.
Because I promised I would always be around.
I would expect no less from you.
Because I know you always exceed everything that I do.
It's always been that way through our fifty years of married life.
That's why I chose you to be my precious wife.
I'm extremely happy that you decided
to share these fifty years with me.
Now the time has come to celebrate our Golden Anniversary.

GOLDEN ANNIVERSARY 2

Thank you for fifty years of being my wife
For the fifty years that I shared in your life.
For the fifty years that I know that you cared.
For the fifty years of joys and sorrows we shared.
Thank you for the fifty years of marital bliss.
Made sweeter each day with every kiss.
But of all the things that I've mentioned above.
I thank you most for the Fifty Years of Love.

ANY YEAR ANNIVERSARY

A wedding is a special thing.
It's more than a bridal walk, a kiss and a ring.
It's a commitment for life,
Between a man and his wife.
It's saying that I truly care,
And that I will always be there.
If you laugh, you know that I'll want to hear.
But if you cry, I'll also shed a tear.
I'll try to lift you up, if you are down.
Because I promised I would always be around.
I would expect no less from you.
Because I know you exceed everything that I do.
It's always been that way throughout our married life.
That's why I chose you to be my precious wife.
Now the time has come to celebrate our Anniversary.
I'm extremely happy that you decided to share these years with me.

ANY YEAR ANNIVERSARY 2

Thank you for being my wife
For the years that I shared in your life.
For the years that I know that you cared.
For the years of joys and sorrows we shared.
Thank you for the years of marital bliss.
Made sweeter each day with every kiss.
But of all the things that I've mentioned above.
I thank you most for these Years of Love.

MISCELLANEOUS ANNIVERSARY VERSES
ANNIVERSARY (hunting analogy)

Sometimes, I may slobber
Or I may even stink.
I'm probably more like a muskrat
Than I am like a mink.
But, in my hunt for my precious wife,
I got me a sable to share my life.

ANNIVERSARY (geese analogy)

Geese are known to mate for life.
That's not always true with a man and a wife.
But I knew that day that I had the first look,
From that day on my goose was cooked.
I hope it has been as good a flight for you as for me.
If so, I hope you enjoy our anniversary.

ANNIVERSARY (enhanced life)

For all these years, you've enhanced my life,
Because you agreed to be my wife.
I can't imagine what my life would be,
If you had not decided to share your life with me.
HAPPY ANNIVERSARY!

MARRIAGE PROPOSAL THANK YOU

Thank you in advance for selecting me to be your wife
For all of the years that I hope to share in your life.
For all of the years that I know that you will care
For all of the joys and sorrows that we will share.
Thank you for what I know will be marital bliss.
Made sweeter each day with every kiss.
But of all the things that I've mentioned above.
I thank you most for your Sweet Love.

WEDDING CONGRATULATIONS CARD

A wedding is a special thing.
It's more than a bridal walk, a kiss and a ring.
 It's a commitment for life,
Between a man and his wife.
Now that you are on the threshold of this life,
I'm sure that you will make a perfect
Husband and wife.

After all of these years, it's still you and me.
The couple that God intended us to be.
For the first years of our life God kept us apart.
But the first time that I saw you, I lost my heart.
I'll have to admit that I tried to get away,
But undying love just made me stay.
So another year has passed, and I'm happy to say.
I hope you also have a HAPPY ANNIVERSARY.

I can't believe we are celebrating another year.
Why in the world am I still around here?
What in the world am I thinking of?
Obviously, it must be true love.

I married the girl I loved, and
I love the woman that I married.

Our days are waning.
We have left but just a few.
That is why each day is special
That I have left with you.

The alphabet has 26 letters,
That we all know thru and thru.
It only takes seven of those letters,
Properly placed and properly spaced.
To say
I LOVE YOU.
HAPPY ANNIVERSARY

A list is a reminder of things that we need to do.

Either shopping, working or whatever is pertinent to you.

A love list is a list of people we love and adore.

Each day it seems that it grows a little bit more.

Personally, I knew from the moment that we first kissed.

That you were moving up fast to the top of MY LOVE LIST.

Happy Anniversary!

Birthdays

A list is a reminder of things that we need to do.

Either shopping, working or whatever is pertinent to you.

A love list is a list of people we love and adore.

Each day it seems that it grows a little bit more.

Personally, I knew from the moment that we first kissed.

That you were moving up fast to the top of MY LOVE LIST.

Happy Birthday!

The alphabet has 26 letters,
That we all know thru and thru.
It only takes seven of those letters,
Properly placed and properly spaced.
To say
I LOVE YOU.
HAPPY BIRTHDAY

Let me tell you about my wildest dreams.

It's something you wouldn't believe.

Of course, my wildest dreams

Are usually something that I wish I could achieve.

Some things in my wildest dreams should be left, not said.

Because, it would probably make you turn a deep crimson red.

From my wildest dreams, I'd better stray away.

So, I'll just wish you a Happy Birthday.

Just as nature has its seasons
You have given me many reasons
To remember many things you did,
When I was only a little kid.
I don't think of those things only on your birthday.
I remember them quite often along the way.
It just tells you the kind of person you are to me.
You will always be special in my memory.
So I'm writing this to you today to say.
I love you, and I hope you have a Happy Birthday.

Your character lines continue to grow.
Shortly, your hair will be white as snow.
Your eyes may not be quite as bright.
Sometimes you have trouble sleeping at night.
But one thing that you getting older does do.
It allows me to wish another
HAPPY BIRTHDAY to you.

Life has four seasons,

As we all know.

I missed most of your spring season,

A long, long time ago.

However, we did get to share,

Our summer and our fall.

Along the whole way,

There were a few bumps and all.

Winter seems to have had a few bigger bumps,

That have gotten in our way.

But just continue to walk and talk with Jesus

And enjoy your senior birthday.

Balloons, fireworks and streamers too.
That's all we need to throw a party for you.
Don't forget the candles and the cake,
Okay, we will use less candles so it won't over-bake.
Suffice it to say that you are umpteen today,
So just enjoy a Happy, Happy Birthday.

There are tears of joy and tears of sorrow.

We will shed only tears of joy for you today and tomorrow.

Not just because God gave us another day.

But because we celebrate another of your birthdays.

Have a HAPPY BIRTHDAY.

I'll give you playing cards for your birthday.

It will just want to make you play and have me pay.

Each time we break open the seal,

You will just say, hurry up, let's deal.

Of course, all of that is no wonder though.

You are just aching to take my dough.

So when we break out these cards and say let's play.

You can remember it as a continual gift from your birthday.

Have a Happy Birthday.

After all of these years, what can I say?
You couldn't be more perfect any other way.
You are the daughter of our dreams
And have achieved a level that most just aspire.
You are the dream that most parents would desire.
When you were born, it was OUR lucky day.
Just enjoy it and have a HAPPY BIRTHDAY.

After all of these years, what can I say?

You couldn't be more perfect any other way.

You are the son of our dreams

And have achieved a level that most just aspire.

You are the dream that most parents would desire.

When you were born, it was OUR lucky day.

Just enjoy it and have a HAPPY BIRTHDAY.

After all of these years, what can I say?
You couldn't be more perfect any other way.
You are the granddaughter of our dreams
And have achieved a level that most just aspire.
You are the dream that most parents would desire.
When you were born, it was OUR lucky day.
Just enjoy it and have a HAPPY BIRTHDAY.

After all of these years, what can I say?
You couldn't be more perfect any other way.
You are the grandson of our dreams
And have achieved a level that most just aspire.
You are the dream that most parents would desire.
When you were born, it was OUR lucky day.
Just enjoy it and have a HAPPY BIRTHDAY.

If we were Romans,

Then we could wear a toga.

If we ate yogurt,

Then we could do yoga.

Although we never did either one,

We did other things to have our fun.

But the greatest thing that we ever got to do,

Was to be the parents of a special daughter like you.

Have a HAPPY BIRTHDAY.

If we were Romans,

Then we could wear a toga.

If we ate yogurt,

Then we could do yoga.

Although we never did either one,

We did other things to have our fun.

But the greatest thing that we ever got to do,

Was to be the parents of a special son like you.

Have a HAPPY BIRTHDAY.

If we were Romans,

Then we could wear a toga.

If we ate yogurt,

Then we could do yoga.

Although we never did either one,

We did other things to have our fun.

But the greatest thing that we ever got to do,

Was to be the grandparents of a special grandson like you.

Have a HAPPY BIRTHDAY.

If we were Romans,
Then we could wear a toga.
If we ate yogurt,
Then we could do yoga.
Although we never did either one,
We did other things to have our fun.
But the greatest thing that we ever got to do,
Was to be the grandparents of a special granddaughter like you.
Have a HAPPY BIRTHDAY.

I said it all, I can't say anymore.

I'm happy because, it's like you live next door.

Without you, I don't know what we would do.

It would be like being in the middle of the ocean

In nothing more than a canoe.

You make our life smooth sailing with all that you do.

It's the love on your part that allows us to be

Dependent on you.

HAVE A HAPPY BIRTHDAY.

I said it all, I can't say anymore.

I'm happy because, it's like you live next door.

Without you, I don't know what I would do.

It would be like being in the middle of the ocean

In nothing more than a canoe.

You make my life smooth sailing with all that you do.

It's the love on your part that allows me to be

Dependent on you.

HAVE A HAPPY BIRTHDAY.

There are things more precious than silver.
There are things more precious than gold.
There are things more precious than money.
At least, that's what I have always been told.
The thing that means more to us,
Than all of the things mentioned above.
Is our precious daughter and all of her precious love.

There are things more precious than silver.
There are things more precious than gold.
There are things more precious than money.
At least, that's what we have always been told.
The thing that means more to us,
Than all of the things mentioned above.
Is our precious son and all of his precious love.

There are things more precious than silver.
There are things more precious than gold.
There are things more precious than money.
At least, that's what I have always been told.
The thing that means more to me,
Than all of the things mentioned above.
Is my precious grandson and all of his precious love.

There are things more precious than silver.
There are things more precious than gold.
There are things more precious than money.
At least, that's what I have always been told.
The thing that means more to me,
Than all of the things mentioned above.
Is my precious granddaughter and all of her precious love.

As I look back through the pictures
That chronicle the events of the past years.
I have to admit that more than one of them
Made me shed some tears.
I wouldn't change any one of them
Anywhere along the way.
So I will just wish my Special Daughter
A Happy, Happy Birthday.

As we look back through the pictures
That chronicle the events of the past years.
We have to admit that more than one of them
Made us shed some tears.
We wouldn't change any one of them
Anywhere along the way.
So we will just wish our Special Son
A Happy, Happy Birthday.

As we look back through the pictures
That chronicle the events of the past years.
We have to admit that more than one of them
Made us shed some tears.
We wouldn't change any one of them
Anywhere along the way.
So we will just wish our Special Grandson
A Happy, Happy Birthday.

As I look back through the pictures
That chronicle the events of the past years.
I have to admit that more than one of them
Made me shed some tears.
I wouldn't change any one of them
Anywhere along the way.
So I will just wish my Special Granddaughter
A Happy, Happy Birthday.

Some years ago, our memories got their start
Of some little girl that totally stole our heart.
If we could verbalize as well as we can visualize
Then sugar, your mind could see.
What this little girl/lovely woman
Has meant to your mom and me.
Since we can't verbalize well enough for you to see
Suffice it to say, our hearts are full of memories.
Have a HAPPY BIRTHDAY.

Some years ago, our memories got their start
Of some little girl that totally stole our heart.
If we could verbalize as well as we can visualize
Then sugar, your mind could see.
What this little girl/lovely woman
Has meant to your dad and me.
Since we can't verbalize well enough for you to see
Suffice it to say, our hearts are full of memories.
Have a HAPPY BIRTHDAY.

Some years ago, our memories got their start
Of some little girl that totally stole our heart.
If we could verbalize as well as we can visualize
Then sugar, your mind could see.
What this little girl/lovely woman
Has meant to your grandpa and me.
Since we can't verbalize well enough for you to see
Suffice it to say, our hearts are full of memories.
Have a HAPPY BIRTHDAY.

Some years ago, our memories got their start
Of some little girl that totally stole our heart.
If we could verbalize as well as we can visualize
Then sugar, your mind could see.
What this little girl/lovely woman
Has meant to your grandma and me.
Since we can't verbalize well enough for you to see
Suffice it to say, our hearts are full of memories.
Have a HAPPY BIRTHDAY.

Some years ago, our memories got their start
Of some little boy that totally stole our heart.
If we could verbalize as well as we can visualize
Then pardner, your mind could see.
What this little boy/handsome man
Has meant to your grandma and me.
Since we can't verbalize well enough for you to see
Suffice it to say, our hearts are full of memories.
Have a HAPPY BIRTHDAY.

Some years ago, our memories got their start
Of some little boy that totally stole our heart.
If we could verbalize as well as we can visualize
Then pardner, your mind could see.
 What this little boy/handsome man
Has meant to your grandpa and me.
Since we can't verbalize well enough for you to see
Suffice it to say, our hearts are full of memories.
Have a HAPPY BIRTHDAY.

Some years ago, our memories got their start
Of some little boy that totally stole our heart.
If we could verbalize as well as we can visualize
Then pardner, your mind could see.
What this little boy/handsome man
Has meant to your mom and me.
Since we can't verbalize well enough for you to see
Suffice it to say, our hearts are full of memories.
Have a HAPPY BIRTHDAY.

Some years ago, our memories got their start
Of some little boy that totally stole our heart.
If we could verbalize as well as we can visualize
Then pardner, your mind could see.
What this little boy/handsome man
Has meant to your dad and me.
Since we can't verbalize well enough for you to see
Suffice it to say, our hearts are full of memories.
Have a HAPPY BIRTHDAY.

Some years ago, my memories got their start
Of some little boy that totally stole my heart.
If I could verbalize as well as I can visualize
Then pardner, your mind could see.
What this little boy/handsome man
Has meant through the years to me.
Since I can't verbalize well enough for you to see
Suffice it to say, my heart is full of memories.
Have a HAPPY BIRTHDAY.

Sweet sixteen is when you really start to change.

You get your driver's license and increase your range.

You have to make more personal decisions along the way.

You have to live by the results of those decisions every day.

So continue to study and get very smart.

Then your decisions will come from your head, not your heart.

So all that is left for Grandma and me to say,

Is we love you and have a HAPPY SIXTEENTH BIRTHDAY.

Sweet sixteen is when you really start to change.

You get your driver's license and increase your range.

You have to make more personal decisions along the way.

You have to live by the results of those decisions every day.

So continue to study and get very smart.

Then your decisions will come from your head, not your heart.

So all that is left for Grandpa and me to say,

Is we love you and have a HAPPY SIXTEENTH BIRTHDAY.

Sweet sixteen is when you really start to change.

You get your driver's license and increase your range.

You have to make more personal decisions along the way.

You have to live by the results of those decisions every day.

So continue to study and get very smart.

Then your decisions will come from your head, not your heart.

So all that is left for Mom and me to say,

Is we love you and have a HAPPY SIXTEENTH BIRTHDAY.

Sweet sixteen is when you really start to change.

You get your driver's license and increase your range.

You have to make more personal decisions along the way.

You have to live by the results of those decisions every day.

So continue to study and get very smart.

Then your decisions will come from your head, not your heart.

So all that is left for Dad and me to say,

Is we love you and have a HAPPY SIXTEENTH BIRTHDAY.

Sweet sixteen is when you really start to change.

You get your driver's license and increase your range.

You have to make more personal decisions along the way.

You have to live by the results of those decisions every day.

So continue to study and get very smart.

Then your decisions will come from your head, not your heart.

So all that is left for me to say,

Is I love you and have a HAPPY SIXTEENTH BIRTHDAY.

I tried to think of
A verse this week
That was as sweet as
A kiss on your cheek.
I just couldn't think
Of anything of that kind,
So I guess you'll think
I'm losing my mind.
Anyway, all I was
Wanting to say
Was I hope you have
A Happy Birthday!

On your birthday, my nerves were about to make me sick.

Finally, your Mama blessed us with a cute little trick.

Our hearts were so full of love and even more,

Because you were the one that we came to adore.

Now all these years later and no longer a teen.

Our love is even sharper and much more keen.

So as you travel along your life's pathway,

Stop for a moment and enjoy your

HAPPY BIRTHDAY.

When you reach the age of twenty-one,
There is a big change for you.
You are now responsible for everything
That you say and you do.
Because we have all watched you mature,
In each and every way.
We have absolutely no worries,
So relax and have a HAPPY BIRTHDAY.

It's your birthday and along the way.

You have made a lot of fond memories for us each day.

Like when you were very young, I took you to shop.

I don't think that I said shop until you drop.

With a basket full of trinkets, I said aren't you through.

You said, just a few more and I think that will do.

You are a star athlete and a scholar as well.

You make our heads and our hearts want to swell.

Don't forget the hugs and kisses along the way.

So before I get too wordy, just let me say.

We wish you an extremely HAPPY BIRTHDAY.

Some years ago today,

A little red head came our way.

She has controlled such a huge part

Of anyone who knows her loving heart.

There are too many memories to delineate today.

So we will just have to say,

We wish her a HAPPY BIRTHDAY.

You always said to keep it simple.

This is as simple as it can be.

To get to where you are,

You just add one to wherever you may be.

I don't know of a simpler way for me to say.

I hope that you have a HAPPY ONE PLUS BIRTHDAY.

If I was going to enhance your stature,

I'll tell you what I would have to do.

I'd have to find another young man,

Exactly like you.

Because you can't improve on perfection

In any other way.

So I will just take this opportunity to wish you,

A HAPPY BIRTHDAY.

If I was going to enhance your stature,
I'll tell you what I would have to do.
I'd have to find another young woman,
Exactly like you.
Because you can't improve on perfection
In any other way.
So I will just take this opportunity to wish you,
A HAPPY BIRTHDAY.

I TRY TO THINK OF A DEFINING MEMORY OF YOUR
FIRST YEARS.
BUT WHEN I DO,
I HAVE TO CHOKE BACK THE TEARS.
WHILE I CAN'T THINK OF ONE PARTICULAR TIME,
I WANT YOU TO KNOW THAT THEY ARE ALL PRECIOUS
MEMORIES OF ALL OF
THE TIMES.
I LOVE YOU.

WE TRY TO THINK OF A DEFINING MEMORY OF
YOUR FIRST YEARS.
BUT WHEN WE DO,
WE HAVE TO CHOKE BACK THE TEARS.
WHILE WE CAN'T THINK OF ONE PARTICULAR TIME,
WE WANT YOU TO KNOW THAT THEY ARE ALL PRE-
CIOUS MEMORIES OF ALL OF
THE TIMES.
WE LOVE YOU.

Who is that coming up the street?
Smiling pretty and looking sweet.
What could I possibly say to her?
Except to sing, there she is Miss America.
One other thing I could possibly say.
I hope you have a HAPPY BIRTHDAY.

Regardless of your goals
Or what you may aspire to be.
You are the personification of perfection
To those who love you, like me.
Whatever your goals are to which you may aspire,
Your ability will always be much, much higher.
Your first young years have already passed away.
But you give us a new memory almost every day.
So here is to you, have a Happy Birthday!

Mom said to write your birthday card in cursive to you this year.

I suggested other ways to write, but she just didn't want to hear.

So I set out to write your birthday card to you today.

The only curse I could think of was,

Hell, I hope that you have a damn nice birthday.

Have a HAPPY BIRTHDAY.

Dad said to write your birthday card in cursive to you this year.

I suggested other ways to write, but she just didn't want to hear.

So I set out to write your birthday card to you today.

The only curse I could think of was,

Hell, I hope that you have a damn nice birthday.

Have a HAPPY BIRTHDAY.

On a California hill, back in forty-nine.

Mr. Sutter was working his mill.

When he made a special find.

It was just a yellow rock, or so it was told.

Until he had it assayed and it was gold.

We were given our gold when you were sent our way.

So we wish you a HAPPY BIRTHDAY.

The corn is turning brown.
The cotton is turning white.
There is a chill in the air,
And a crispness in the night.
It reminds us that it is autumn
And it is time for us to say.
We wish our special grandchild,
A HAPPY BIRTHDAY.

The corn is turning brown.
The cotton is turning white.
There is a chill in the air,
And a crispness in the night.
It reminds us that it is autumn
And it is time for us to say.
We wish our special child,
A HAPPY BIRTHDAY.

1 times 24 = 1 day

7 times 24 = 1 week

365 times 24 = 1 year

Several years times 365 times 24 = a lot of hours

That equals our grandchild's umpteenth birthday.

Oh! I almost forgot to add

umpteen times 24 for the leap years.

Oh Well! HAPPY UMPTEENTH BIRTHDAY anyway.

1 times 24 = 1 day

7 times 24 = 1 week

365 times 24 = 1 year

umpteenth times 365 times 24 = a lot of hours

That equals our child's umpteenth birthday.

Oh! I almost forgot to add

3 times 24 for the leap years.

Oh Well! Have a HAPPY UMPTEENTH BIRTHDAY anyway!

If we could order a grandson from heaven up above.

The first requirement would be one that we could love.

We'd ask that he be big, strong, courteous and handsome, you see.

And we wouldn't mind if he acted a little like his Grandma and me…

Some years ago today, our prayers were answered and we were blessed.

We got a grandson that exceeded all of our requests.

So "pardner", know that we love you, and just wanted to say.

We wish you happiness on your BIRTHDAY.

If we could order a grandson from heaven up above.

The first requirement would be one that we could love.

We'd ask that he be big, strong, courteous and handsome, you see.

And we wouldn't mind if he acted a little like his Grandpa and me…

Some years ago today, our prayers were answered and we were blessed.

We got a grandson that exceeded all of our requests.

So sugar, know that we love you, and just wanted to say.

We wish you happiness on your BIRTHDAY.

If we could order a son from heaven up above.

The first requirement would be one that we could love.

We'd ask that he be big, strong, courteous and handsome, you see.

And we wouldn't mind if he acted a little like his Mom and me…

Some years ago today, our prayers were answered and we were blessed.

We got a son that exceeded all of our requests.

So pardner, know that we love you, and just wanted to say.

We wish you happiness on your BIRTHDAY.

If we could order a son from heaven up above.

The first requirement would be one that we could love.

We'd ask that he be big, strong, courteous and handsome, you see.

And we wouldn't mind if he acted a little like his Dad and me...

Some years ago today, our prayers were answered and we were blessed.

We got a son that exceeded all of our requests.

So sugar, know that we love you, and just wanted to say.

We wish you happiness on your BIRTHDAY.

A birthday is a special event.
You wonder what is ahead and
Where last year went.
God does have it all planned for you.
Someday, you will understand
What he wants you to do.
But don't worry about it on this,
Your special day.
Just enjoy your Happy Birthday.

Today you are considered an adult and a man.

Freedom and responsibility come with whatever you plan.

Your plan will make us proud of anything that you do.

If you will take the time to think your plan through.

It's been a pleasure to watch you grow to where you are.

It's just the beginning and we know you will go far.

Whatever your plan is and whatever you do.

Remember that we will always love you.

We wish you a HAPPY BIRTHDAY.

Today you are considered an adult and a woman.

Freedom and responsibility come with whatever you plan.

Your plan will make us proud of anything that you do.

If you will take the time to think your plan through.

It's been a pleasure to watch you grow to where you are.

It's just the beginning and we know you will go far.

Whatever your plan is and whatever you do.

Remember that we will always love you.

We wish you a HAPPY BIRTHDAY.

She is my favorite little girl;
In all of the world.
She is my sugar booger bear
With the pretty head of hair
She is my sweety tweety pie
 And is the apple of my eye.
She is a year or two older today.
And I want this to say,
Have a HAPPY BIRTHDAY!

Watching a Hawaiian sunset with you is really something to see.
Or going to the mountains and watching a full day of snow with me.
Or maybe it was going to Europe and seeing much more.
But these were just a few of the things that we adore.
I'm extremely glad that you shared most of your years with me.
So I hope that you will have a
HAPPY BIRTHDAY.

When you think you need a kiss.
Here is all you have to do.
Just close your birthday card,
And I'll be kissing you.
Happy Birthday

IN MY WILDEST DREAMS,

I was driving down Country Rd.

When I saw a bicycle carrying a heavy load.

I decided that I had better pull over and stop.

The tires looked like they were about to pop.

I thought, who in the world could this possibly be?

Why, it looked like an old friend to me.

So I rolled down the window and yelled her way.

Hey, OLD GIRL, I hope you have a

HAPPY BIRTHDAY.

All of these years of adoration
For the prettiest woman in the nation
I'm just happy that God sent you my way
So today I could wish you a Happy Birthday

Some years ago today, your Mother had a bundle of joy.

We were ecstatic to hear that it was a little boy.

We started to hugging you and kissing your cheeks until they were red.

Grandma would kiss your other cheeks

when she changed your diapers on the bed.

I always stayed away from that other end.

Because, I didn't know if it was still loaded or when it was full of wind.

But just because you turned a year older today,

It doesn't mean that we can't hug and kiss you anyway.

Before I lose my chain of thought, let me say.

We hope you HAVE A HAPPY BIRTHDAY.

Doggy-Themed Birthday verse

Arf, arf, bow, wow and howl or two
That's the way a doggie says
Happy Birthday to you.
I'm not a doggie but I wanted you to see,
An extra special Happy Birthday
Wish from me.

22nd Birthday Verse

When you were little, you had a tutu;
As cute as it could be.
You would dance around and prance around,
For all of the family to see.
Now we have all gotten older,
And the story that I will tell.
Now you have a different two-two,
Which fits you perfectly well.
Have a HAPPY 22nd BIRTHDAY.

Lottery Scratch-Off -Themed Birthday Verse

For your birthday, here is a little present for you.

It's just a little ticket that requires a scratch or two.

If you happen to be lucky, you might have a big win.

If you don't win with the first one, just try again.

If you just happen to have one that does win the big dough.

It's only right that you share with the people you know.

HAVE A HAPPY BIRTHDAY.

Miscellaneous

A LETTER FROM A SOLDIER

Some years ago, in another war, halfway around the world.
A lonely First Lieutenant was thinking of his wife and little girl.
She was only eighteen months young and as sweet as she could be.
This was at Christmas time and just her second tree.
Her mom had decorated to perfection, as she always did.
This soldier was aching just to hug his little kid.
But it was not to be, so he sat down with his pen.
He wrote this little poem, until they could be together again.

Christmas, Oh Christmas.
Must you be so cruel?
The time of joy, the time of cheer,
The season of good yule.

It seems so sad for me to know,
There will be no holly or mistletoe.
The smell of cedars so crisp and clear,
Will be but a vision to me this year.

A tiny girl so sweet to me,
Will be enjoying her second Christmas tree.
With bulbs so shiny and lights so bright,
Oh! To see her face on Christmas night.

Or to see the joy in her mother's eyes.
When on Christmas morning, she hears her cry.
Mommy, Mommy come and see.
What Santa Claus has brought to me.

But Christmas, as you can easily see.
These visions will at least be with me.
Although I may not be there to take part.
I will be there in mind and heart.

Christmas, oh Christmas.
Must you be so cruel?
The time of joy, the time of cheer,
The season of good yule.
It seems so sad for me to know,
There will be no holly or mistletoe.
The smell of cedars so crisp and clear,
Will be but a vision to me this year.

A tiny boy so sweet to me,
Will be enjoying one of his early Christmas trees.
With bulbs so shiny and lights so bright,
Oh! To see his face on Christmas night.

Or to see the joy in his mother's eyes.
When on Christmas morning, she hears him cry.
Mommy, Mommy come and see.
What Santa Claus has brought to me.

But Christmas, as you can easily see.
These visions will at least be with me.
Although I may not be there to take part.
I will be there in mind and heart.

Christmas, Oh Christmas.
Must you be so cruel?
The time of joy, the time of cheer,
The season of good yule.

It seems so sad for me to know,
There will be no holly or mistletoe.
The smell of cedars so crisp and clear,
Will be but a vision to me this year.
A tiny girl so sweet to me,
Will be enjoying one of her early Christmas trees.
With bulbs so shiny and lights so bright,
Oh! To see her face on Christmas night.

Or to see the joy in her mother's eyes.
When on Christmas morning, she hears her cry.
Mommy, Mommy come and see.
What Santa Claus has brought to me.

But Christmas, as you can easily see.
These visions will at least be with me.
Although I may not be there to take part.
I will be there in mind and heart.

A THANK YOU TO TEACHERS

You helped to nurture my children along.
And with each group of kids, it was the same song.
To let you know that I appreciate what you do.
I wanted to send this note to the teachers like you.
Of course, my kids are not as special to you as they are to me.
But I know all of the kids at your school are as special as they can be.
So keep nurturing and sending them along.
It will help our country to continue to stay strong.
Somewhere, down the road, the kids from your school will say.
My school helped to shape me and make me turn out this way.

A CHRISTMAS GATHERING

T'was the night before Christmas, as it used to be…

And it was time for another family Christmas tree.

Grandma and Grandpa were sitting in their chair.

And it seemed like presents were stacked everywhere.

Usually, Grandpa would say a few words and a prayer.

Then pandemonium would break out around there.

People were sitting everywhere you could see.

In chairs, on the stair, or on Mom or Dad's knee.

Paper started flying and bows everywhere.

Cause the easiest way to open a gift was to give it a tear.

By the time it was over, paper was knee high.

And there was so much noise, you couldn't hear a baby cry.

The paper would be gathered to be tossed in the trash barrel outside.

No telling how many presents went along on that ride.

The kids were all loaded with many a toy.

Once again, you could say we had a real Christmas joy.

As the party broke up and we would leave that night.

Everyone was wishing a Merry Christmas and have a good night.

Graduation

Your graduation is justification for our jubilation.

Your graduation doesn't create any more exultation.

You have always been the personification of our admiration.

So this is just an abbreviation in the culmination

of your quest for an education.

Your college degree is our expectation.

We will cheer at your degree's culmination.

Congratulations on your graduation.

But always remember you have our greatest admiration.

Even more, you have our total adoration.

As a surrogate for your granddaddy
I guess it's left up to me.
To tell you how proud
Your granddaddy would be.
To see his beautiful granddaughter
About to become a blushing bride.
Being ushered down the aisle
With her proud daddy by her side.
In my mind, he is probably
Watching from above.
Through me, as his surrogate,
He sends the two of you his love.

A GREAT LIFE

You've had your fights and your strife.

But you also had your joys and laughter in your life.

But let's not talk about what your life is, or used to be.

Let's just talk about you and your posterity and your family tree.

You've been a mother and a wife too,

And a grandmother, and who knows, before it's all through.

All of these people who are in your line,

who knows what they will be?

Some may be renowned or may even change history.

But regardless of what their plight might be,

They will all owe a debt of gratitude to a mother, grandmother or

The great, great-great etc., in their history.

So now that you are in this current strife,

Think of all of the people affected by GOD'S gift of YOUR GREAT LIFE.

My understanding of EMPATHY is:

When you have walked that trail that the other is walking,

When you have experienced the loss that the other is experiencing,

When you have felt the hurt that the other is feeling…

Then you can truly say that you empathize with the other.

I wanted you to know that you are in my thoughts

and prayers and I ask that God

Grant you peace and comfort at this traumatic time.

Your friend.

OLD MAN IN I.C.U.

THE OLD MAN LAID THERE IN THE I.C.U.
IF HE COULD HAVE TALKED, HE WOULD HAVE SAID
THERE IS SOMETHING
THAT I HAVE TO DO.
IT'S SUNDAY. AND I'VE MISSED CHURCH FOR TWO
WEEKS IN A ROW.
I'VE GOT TO GET OUT OF HERE, SO THAT I CAN GO.
AND THIS MORNING AS HE PASSED THROUGH THAT
HEAVENLY DOOR.
HE SAID, "PRAISE GOD, IT'S SUNDAY," AND I WON'T
MISS CHURCH ANY MORE.

OLD WOMAN IN I.C.U.

THE OLD WOMAN LAID THERE IN THE I.C.U.
IF SHE COULD HAVE TALKED, SHE WOULD HAVE
SAID THERE IS SOMETHINGTHAT I HAVE TO DO.
IT'S SUNDAY. AND I'VE MISSED CHURCH FOR TWO
WEEKS IN A ROW.
I'VE GOT TO GET OUT OF HERE, SO THAT I CAN GO.
AND THIS MORNING AS SHE PASSED THROUGH
THAT HEAVENLY DOOR.
SHE SAID, "PRAISE GOD, IT'S SUNDAY," AND I WON'T
MISS CHURCH ANY MORE.

PRINCIPLES ARE ONE THING,
AND PRINCIPALS ARE ANOTHER.
ONE TELLS YOU HOW TO ACT,
THE OTHER CAN TREAT YOU LIKE A MOTHER.
IF YOU DO GOOD SHE WILL TELL AND ENCOURAGE YOU,
AND THEN LET YOU GO.
BUT IF YOU DO BAD, YOU CAN BET THAT SHE WILL LET YOU KNOW!
PRINCIPLES THAT YOU HAVE TAUGHT THEM,
THEY WILL APPLY THROUGHOUT THEIR LIVES.
EITHER IN THE IR OCCUPATIONS,
OR AS HUSBANDS AND/OR WIVES.
SO THE STUDENTS OF YOUR SCHOOL ARE LUCKY, AS YOU CAN SEE.
TO HAVE HAD YOU AS THEIR PRINCIPAL, TO SHOW THEM HOW THEY SHOULD BE.

PRINCIPLES ARE ONE THING,
AND PRINCIPALS ARE ANOTHER.
ONE TELLS YOU HOW TO ACT,
THE OTHER CAN TREAT YOU LIKE A FATHER.
IF YOU DO GOOD HE WILL TELL AND ENCOURAGE YOU,
AND THEN LET YOU GO.
BUT IF YOU DO BAD, YOU CAN BET THAT HE WILL LET YOU KNOW!
PRINCIPLES THAT YOU HAVE TAUGHT THEM,
THEY WILL APPLY THROUGHOUT THEIR LIVES.
EITHER IN THEIR OCCUPATIONS,
OR AS HUSBANDS AND/OR WIVES.
SO THE STUDENTS OF YOUR SHCOOL ARE LUCKY, AS YOU CAN SEE.
TO HAVE HAD YOU AS THEIR PRINCIPAL,
TO SHOW THEM HOW THEY SHOULD BE.

A quilt can comfort, shield and protect you
And add beauty too.
It's ironic how it parallels
God's love for me and you.
Quilts can cover our world
Like God can cover our life
The patchwork pattern of the quilt
Are like life's joys and strife
A quilt has many styles,
The pattern is up to you.
Just as God allows the pattern of our life
To be determined by what we say and do.
However, God did give us a pattern
To help us learn how to pray
It's called the Lord 's Prayer
And it should be said at least once a day.

Our Father, which art in heaven
Hallowed be thy name.
Thy kingdom come.
Thy will be done in earth,
As it is in heaven.
Give us this day
Our daily bread.
And forgive us our debts,
As we forgive those who ate debtors.
And lead us not into temptation,
But deliver us from evil:
For thine is the kingdom,
And the power,
And the glory,
Forever,
Amen.

Tears of jubilation
Stream down on our face.
It's because we had a graduation
Just happen around this place.
You probably have as much jubilation
As anyone that you see.
Because this is an accomplishment
Which should make you extremely happy.
Congratulations,
We all love you.

You no longer have our grandchildren
Under your care.
But I wanted to let you know
What a positive influence you had on them there.
So as our grandchildren are moving on
And bid you a fond *Adieu*.

Just think of all of the other children
That were positively influenced by you.
Best wishes and thanks for a job well done.

Sometimes, the tooth fairy seems unkind.
He forgets to leave money at the proper time.
But when he remembers, as you can see.
He leaves the money, with his apology.

We Love You,
The Tooth Fairy

It's the first morning without you and I can already tell.

That around here, it's going to be lonesome as ——!

For you, it's a trip back to home,

To spend a few days with your family alone.

I know that it's work that had to be done.

But I hope you can relax and at least have some fun.

Don't worry about me, I'll be just fine.

I just wanted to vent and to whine.

Also, I wanted to say.

I love you and hope you enjoy each and every day.

Daughter's Reprimand

I knew what you were saying
When you were reprimanding me.
I did something questionable
That challenged my ability.
Although you were quite vocal,
I knew what you were trying to say,
Was I Love You Dad and I didn't want
You to die today.

College Graduation verse

This graduation is justification for our jubilation.

This graduation does create more exultation.

You have always been the personification of our admiration

So this is the ultimate in the culmination of your quest for an education.

Your college degree was our expectation.

We will cheer because of your degree's culmination.

Congratulations on your graduation.

But always remember you have our greatest admiration.

Even more, you have our total adoration.

Now, who knows what life has in store.

Don't worry, just relax and enjoy the hula a little more.

When you return, then start opening life's opportunity door.

Infinite Love

As we all know, life is finite.

When we leave here, there still will be things to do.

I wanted you to know that my infinite love

Will travel through eternity for you.

Marriage Proposal Thank You (Male Version)

Thank you in advance for being my wife;
For all of the years that I hope to share in your life,
For all of the years that I know that you will care,
For all of the joys and sorrows that we will share.
Thank you for what I know will be marital bliss,
Made sweeter each day with every kiss.
But of all the things that I mentioned above,
I thank you most for your Sweet Love.

Matches

Matches are made to use to light a fire.
But some matches are made in heaven
To fulfill someone's desire.

Mother's Day

Have you ever thought of the plight of a
Mother to be.
She is first a little girl that sat on your knee.
But in no time at all, along comes a guy
That just happens to be the one that catches her eye.
Shortly then, you will have a bad day,
Because this guy will marry her and take her away.
Then comes a bundle of joy that gives you glee
It's a baby whose mother was the little girl that used to
Sit on your knee.
Have a Happy Mother's Day

You are not my mother.

It was not up to you.

But because you worry,

And do the things you do.

You take care of me,

Kind of in a mother's way.

So I'm giving you,

This special wish today.

Have a Happy Mother's Day.

Any woman can bear a child,
But not all women can be a mother.
It means sacrificing your wants and desires
To the wishes and needs of another.
Being a mother is ordained from above
But you are the one that adds the Love.

Explaining what a mother is,

Would be hard to define.

It's hard to encapsulate the definition

In just a few lines

To sum it up in a few words,

The best that you can do.

Is to say, a mother means someone,

Who has unconditional love for you.

HAVE A HAPPY MOTHER'S DAY.

Mom, you know that it is Mother's Day.
I have something that I want to say.
You've been my mother every day,
Each and every day, my whole life through.
That is why I wanted to emphatically state,
Mom, I Love You.

A mother is a woman,
That's absolute and true.
She is the person,
That will love and care for you.
Of all the other things,
That God included from above.
He made a mother the absolute
Personification of Love.

The saying is you lead by example,
As you have surely done.
I know that you wanted more children
At least you were blessed with a special one.
She was always watching,
Just to see what you would do.
So now you have a daughter
Exactly like you.
As a mother, you led her to be that way.
So, sit back, relax, and enjoy a special
Mother's day.

Vicariously means living through your imagination,
Someone else's hurts, aches, accomplishments and dreams.
A mother experiences these things twice as much.
But she can offer comfort or pride with just a simple touch.
That's why this day was set aside just to honor you.
Even though we should honor you, the whole year through.
Have a HAPPY MOTHER'S DAY.

Food Gift on Mother's Day Verse

Here is a little gift made just for you.

To remind you of the things that your mama used to do.

While you are eating it, think of her up above.

With each little bite a remembrance of her love.

Mother's Day without Your Mother Verse

Remember the little gifts from your mother,
And the things that she would make for you.
She has long since passed, and now is living above.
But here is a little gift to remind you of her Love.

Another Mother's Day without Your Mother Verse

Whether your mother is living,
Or gone on to live above.
A mother is God's way
Of defining what is LOVE?

Valentine's Day

As I listen to you breathing softly while you lay there and rest.
I think how lucky I am to have married the very best.
I have always been happy to claim you as mine,
Especially to claim you as my lifetime VALENTINE.

This makes another HAPPY VALENTINE for you and me,
That I have had the pleasure of you sharing with me.
So, I thought I would write this little line,
To say that I'm glad you are still my SPECIAL VALENTINE.

If I had a set of antlers.

I know what I would do.

I'd twist them into the shape of a heart.

That would be my VALENTINE for you.

Since I don't have any antlers, or a deer on the way.

I'll just have to wish you a Happy VALENTINE's day.

IF IT WAS EASTER, I'D DRAW YOU A RABBIT.
IF IT WAS HALLOWEEN, I'D DRAW YOU A PUMPKIN.
IF IT WAS CHRISTMAS, I'D DRAW YOU A CHRISTMAS TREE.
BUT I DON'T NEED TO DRAW YOU A HARE,
A PUMPKIN OR A PINE,
I'LL DRAW YOU A BIG HEART AND SAY THAT I'M
GLAD YOU'RE MY
VALENTINE.

A gold miner will look for a nugget,
And doesn't know where it will be.
But I found my gold nugget,
When you came to be with me.
Just as a nugget has such a pretty shine,
I will always shine because you are my Valentine.

Words can't describe the love we have for you.

Although we don't always agree with everything that you do.

But all of our memories of you will always continue to shine.

Because you are our SPECIAL VALENTINE.

If I was a monkey,
Swinging in a tree.
I'd be a happy monkey
If you were swinging
There with me.
Since I'm not a monkey,
It suits me just fine,
Because you will always be,
My Special Valentine.

My VALENTINE wish is that all of your dreams will come true.

But if that can't happen right away for you.

I want you to know that everything will be just fine.

As long as you continue to be my VALENTINE.

We want to make this note CONCISE and CLEAR.
It is for one very special little dear.
We think that she is extremely fine.
Therefore, we want her to be our
SPECIAL VALENTINE.

Valentine is a time to express our love.

As you know, God sent his love on the wings of a dove.

If we used that symbol of our love for you,

One little dove would just not do.

So picture a drove of doves, so white and so fine,

And know that you are our Very Special VALENTINE.

Valentine is a day when you want to say,
How much you love someone every day.
So I guess that today, that it is time,
To tell you that you are our Special Valentine.

Trying to make a Valentine card for someone like you,
Is something that is really hard to do.
You are a muscular teenager and a handsome dude too.
So the best that I can do is say HAPPY VALENTINE to you.

Jams, Jellies and Sugar, all three,
Are not as sweet as you are to
Grandma and me.
When we think of sweet,
The best thought we can find,
Is our granddaughter,
Our Sweet Valentine.

A bouquet of roses is beautiful,
But soon they wilt away.
A box of candy is sweet,
But it lasts for just a few days.
But you, my darling, have stood
The proverbial test of time.
Because you are still
My Precious Valentine.

You know the old story.

Roses are red and violets are blue.

But with the beauty of the season,

There comes the AC…CHOO!

But the beauty of the year is when we get to say.

We wish our Extra Special Valentine,

A Happy Valentine Day.

When you hear the rooster crowing
His *cock-a-doodle-do*.
You know he is just crowing
We love you.
If he would just finish his crowing,
It would suit us just fine.
If he would just crow we love you,
OUR SPECIAL VALENTINE.

If you were a boy,
Just turning into the time of men.
You probably would not want to hear this
Over and over again.
But you are going to hear it at least
This one more time.
Because Grandma and Grandpa still
Claim you as our SPECIAL VALENTINE.

What do you say to your valentine,
That you haven't said before?
Except to say that I love you and
You are the person that I adore.
Although a few trials have came our way,
You are still my valentine each and every day.

You have had a bad year,
 But you've handled it my dear.
Your strength I adore
And so much more.
You didn't just sit around and whine
So I'm happy to say that you are
My Special Valentine.

There is an angel among us,
And she lives nearby.
Since we love her to death,
You understand the reason why.
She is her mom's and mine,
And we will always claim her
As our EXTRA SPECIAL VALENTINE.

I've said it before and I will say it again.
The only way we could have had more love and care
Would be for you to have been a twin.
But God heaped all of our blessings in our special girl.
He gave us the most special VALENTINE that can
Be found in the whole world.

When you Google Valentine,
The meaning is really quite clear.
It's someone very special,
For whom your love is very dear.
That definition seems to work for us,
Perfectly, all of the time.
Because, for us, you will always be,
Our SPECIAL VALENTINE.

He is tall, handsome and muscular, you see.
He is as nice as any teenage boy can be.
His six pack has sort of drained away.
But we will talk about that some other day.
Grandma and I think he is extremely fine.
So we want to claim him as our
SPECIAL VALENTINE.

You don't give a man toys.
That's for little boys.
They prefer things that make noise.
Like trucks, guns and 4 wheelers are just fine.
But all we are going to give you is hugs and
Kisses and call you our
SPECIAL VALENTINE.

If I Could Text a Valentine

If I could text, I know what I would do.
I'd text a picture of a heart and I'd send it to you.
I'd simply say I Love You on the next line
And then claim you as my Special VALENTINE.

Daughter as a Valentine

Since I have a daughter
Who is so sweet and kind.
I simply have to say
You are my special VALENTINE.

Special Valentine

Since you are who you are,
This is really not hard to do.
Because most people would like
To have a valentine like you
Since I don't say it all of the time,
I want you to know that you are
My special VALENTINE.